D1710120

The ultimate study companion to Picmonic for Nursing is here! Our 4 Weeks to NCLEX® Picmonic Workbook & Study Planner is our latest brain baby designed to help prep you for the NCLEX® like a boss.

At Picmonic, we're masters of memorizing. By using our online app along with this plan, you'll be on your way to test success!

In this workbook you'll find:

- A study plan broken down by week
- Fun review games
- Full color HD images
- A high-yield playlist complete with study hacks
- Coloring book pages

This is a companion workbook to the Picmonic for Nursing subscription, available at Picmonic.com, and does not include story, text, quizzes, or other features that replace the course. This workbook is to be used in conjunction with the Picmonic web and mobile apps, and is not a replacement for the apps.

Have feedback for us? Please don't hesitate to shoot an email to feedback@picmonic.com and let us know what you think!

Cheers,

The Picmonic Team

TABLE OF CONTENTS

Hello Future Nurse!

WOO! You made it this far; go ahead and pinch yourself, pat yourself on the back, and yell *hallelujah* to the sky. Because my friends, you have climbed the huge mountain that is nursing school, and you've arrived at the top!

Now, as you are reading this, you are probably trying to figure out the best way to prepare to take the biggest exam of your nursing career. Fortunately, you've found Picmonic, and we are here to help you crush that exam!

As a company made by students for students, we understand the roller coaster of emotions that you are going through. We're in constant contact with the thousands of students who use our product, taking all your input into consideration to make the best study tool to suit your needs.

I'll admit this to you all; at the beginning of nursing school, I was a crammer. The night before a big exam, I would pull an all-nighter, frantically searching through my books and notes. The next morning for the exam I would arrive, in an over-caffeinated daze, take the test, and walk out forgetting everything I had learned the night before. One day I realized this had to stop. I knew I needed to retain this information for the long-run; not to just pass my classes, but to become a successful, competent nurse.

That's when I discovered Picmonic, and I very quickly realized what an incredibly powerful tool was at my fingertips. I was amazed at how simple it was for me to learn even the most difficult concepts. I could master a whole chapter of information in less than five minutes, all while laughing my head off at the outrageous Picmonic characters and hilarious stories.

By taking the stress out of studying, it no longer became a heavy burden. Although the NCLEX® seems to be one of the biggest stress inducers for nursing students, we want to alleviate that anxiety and show you that it can be manageable, even, dare I say, fun. You'll see that by using this 4-Week Study Planner we've created, you can customize your personal daily routine based on your own study habits. We know everyone is different, so we've designed this schedule so you are able to work at your own pace, stopping to review when needed, or taking a moment to answer 50+ extra practice questions from other resources to reinforce the content.

You'll also find that we've included lots of tips help you along the way. Use this advice to fit your needs and learn from those that have been there before. By following this study plan, you will know that you are ready to pass the NCLEX® the first time; we even guarantee it.

Now, get ready for the adventure ahead, and remember: study less, remember more.

Marlee Liberman, RN
Picmonic's Master Nursing Scholar

HOW TO USE PICMONIC

Picmonic turns the facts you're learning in nursing school and turns them into fun and memorable stories that you'll never forget. With the Picmonic learning system, you'll master everything you need to pass the NCLEX®.

Using Picmonic is as easy as 1 2 3!

1. **Create a Picmonic Account**   2. **Play Picmonics**   3. **Lock it in with Daily Quizzes**

Start watching Picmonics today by visiting **picmonic.com** or use the **QR code**

Be sure to find an additional QR code for the "Top 100 Picmonics for NCLEX" playlist on page 36!

HOW TO USE THIS PLANNER

We know that not everyone will be taking the NCLEX® at the same time, so we've taken all of the information presented and spread it out through a 4-week, time-manageable schedule, allowing you to tailor your study sessions to your own individual needs. We want you to feel empowered to use this planner as a tool to get your studying in while actually allowing yourself to have a normal life (crazy, right!?

Our study sessions last anywhere from 30 minutes to just over 4 hours. It's all about versatility here. Can you stack days on top of each other? Absolutely. Should you? Well, that's on you. If the content is too much, or you feel burnt out, maybe it's time to take a break or call it a day. The main idea is knowing what to expect time commitment wise and plan ahead. This way, you're not cramming until 3am the night prior. As with any deadline, the sooner you begin, the easier time you'll have.

Picmonic offers a lot of content that will assist you in making sure those hard-to-retain, must-know important facts remain with you come NCLEX® time. That's why we've also taken webinars from our Picmonic Lecture Series and incorporated them into the 4-Week Study Planner when relevant.

Imagine that the NCLEX® is a marathon... a marathon of questions. And you wouldn't run a marathon without training first. We suggest selecting a practice question bank that allows you to separate questions into subject areas. You'll need to practice as many questions as possible before your exam date, and we suggest doing intervals of 50-55 questions each day. We recommend doing a total of 1,500 questions in addition to Picmonic. If you aren't mastering the questions then you may need to do as many as 2,500-3,000 before you're considered a master.

CALENDAR

SUNDAY	MONDAY	TUESDAY	WEDNESDAY	THURSDAY	FRIDAY	SATURDAY

WEEK 1

Dates: _____

MY GOAL THIS WEEK IS TO DO 150 PRACTICE QUESTIONS

THINGS I NEED TO WORK ON:

1. _____
2. _____
3. _____
4. _____
5. _____

ADVICE: Don't skip high-yield content and "hope" you don't get questions about it. You probably will and we want you to stay calm.

Besides, there's probably a Picmonic for that.

DAY 1 ☐

TODAY'S FOCUS

6am	
7am	
8am	
9am	
10am	
11am	
12pm	
1pm	
2pm	
3pm	
4pm	
5pm	
6pm	
7pm	
8pm	
9pm	
10pm	
11pm	
12am	

PATHWAY: Fundamental Review > Nursing Basics
61 PICMONICS: 3HRS 50MINS
☐ Nursing Basics (3)
☐ Assessments and Vital Signs (7)
☐ Communication (3)
☐ Culture (5)
☐ Lung Sounds (4)
☐ General Tests and Procedures (7)
☐ Lab Values (32)

Webinars:
☐ Tips and Tricks to Mastering NCLEX-Style Questions
☐ Fundamental Concepts

DAY 2 ☐

TODAY'S FOCUS

6am	
7am	
8am	
9am	
10am	
11am	
12pm	
1pm	
2pm	
3pm	
4pm	
5pm	
6pm	
7pm	
8pm	
9pm	
10pm	
11pm	
12am	

PATHWAY: Fundamental Review > Foundations for Practice
11 PICMONICS: 55MINS
☐ Patient Safety (6)
☐ Infection Prevention & Control (4)
☐ Delegation (1)

> Perioperative Care
6 PICMONICS: 35MINS
☐ Perioperative Care (4)
☐ Drain & Device Care (2)

DAY 3 ☐

TODAY'S FOCUS

6am	
7am	
8am	
9am	
10am	
11am	
12pm	
1pm	
2pm	
3pm	
4pm	
5pm	
6pm	
7pm	
8pm	
9pm	
10pm	
11pm	
12am	

PATHWAY: Pharmacology Basics > Medication Administration
9 PICMONICS: 45MINS
☐ Basics of Medication Administration (3)
☐ Routes of Administration (2)
☐ Medication Administration (4)

> Pharmacology Basics
25 PICMONICS: 2HRS 5MINS
☐ G Protein Coupled Receptors (2)
☐ P450 Interactions (2)
☐ Toxicities & Reversal Agents (13)

Webinar:
☐ Pharm: Know Your Endings (Parts 1-3)

TODAY'S FOCUS

6am	
7am	
8am	
9am	
10am	
11am	
12pm	
1pm	
2pm	
3pm	
4pm	
5pm	
6pm	
7pm	
8pm	
9pm	
10pm	
11pm	
12am	

PATHWAY: Fluid, Electrolyte, & Acid Base Imbalances > Fluid Imbalances
5 PICMONICS: 25MINS
☐ Infusion Therapies (5)
> Electrolytes
19 PICMONICS: 1HR 35MINS
☐ Electrolyte Lab Values (7)
☐ Electrolyte Imbalances (12)
☐ Acid Base Imbalances (9)

Webinars:
☐ Master Acid Base Like a Pro

TODAY'S FOCUS

6am	
7am	
8am	
9am	
10am	
11am	
12pm	
1pm	
2pm	
3pm	
4pm	
5pm	
6pm	
7pm	
8pm	
9pm	
10pm	
11pm	
12am	

PATHWAY: Respiratory System > Assessments
13 PICMONICS: 1HR 5MINS
☐ Respiratory Assessments (5)
☐ Lung Sounds (4)
☐ Oxygenation (4)

> Disorders
21 PICMONICS: 1 HR 45 MINS
☐ Respiratory Disorders (21)

> Pharmacology
7 PICMONICS: 35 MINS
☐ Anti-TB Medications (2)
☐ Respiratory Pharmacology (5)

TODAY'S FOCUS

6am	
7am	
8am	
9am	
10am	
11am	
12pm	
1pm	
2pm	
3pm	
4pm	
5pm	
6pm	
7pm	
8pm	
9pm	
10pm	
11pm	
12am	

PATHWAY: Cardiovascular System > Assessments
8 PICMONICS: 40MINS
☐ ECG (5)
☐ Cardiac Enzymes (3)
Webinar:
☐ ECG/EKG Review

> Disorders
41 PICMONICS: 3HRS 20MINS
☐ Hypertension & Hypotension (6)
☐ Angina (2)
☐ Myocardial Infarction (5)
☐ Heart Failure (4)
☐ Inflammatory Heart Conditions (7)
☐ Heart Murmurs & Malformations (7)
☐ Vascular Disorders (7)
☐ Shock & Sepsis (3)
Webinar:
☐ Blood Flow and Heart Failure Rapid Review

TODAY'S FOCUS

6am	
7am	
8am	
9am	
10am	
11am	
12pm	
1pm	
2pm	
3pm	
4pm	
5pm	
6pm	
7pm	
8pm	
9pm	
10pm	
11pm	
12am	

PATHWAY: Cardiovascular System
> Pharmacology
24 PICMONICS: 2HRS
☐ Antihypertensives (9)
☐ Antiarrhythmics (4)
☐ Inotropes (5)
☐ Dyslipidemia Medications (6)

WEEK 1 ACTIVITIES

1. Fill in the Blank

1. The normal range for potassium (K+) is typically __3.5__ to __5.1__.

2. In the Glasgow Coma Scale (GCS), a score of __15__ is the highest awarded to a fully alert person; the lowest possible score is __3__. A GCS of less than __8__ often indicates coma.

3. The normal pulse rate for an adult ranges from __60__ to __100__ beats per minute.

4. The normal range for calcium (Ca2+) is typically __8.5__ to __10.5__

5. The contrast that is used with an MRI ~~does~~ / does not pose a risk to patients with iodine or shellfish allergies (circle one).

6. In Maslow's hierarchy of needs, the base of the pyramid is labeled __Physiological__ needs.

7. The normal range for sodium (Na+) is typically __135__ to __145__.

8. __neutrophils__ are the primary acting leukocytes in the body.

9. The normal hemoglobin (Hgb) lab values in men typically range from __13__ to __17__, and for women typically range from __12__ to __16__.

10. Patients on airborne precautions should be placed in a __negative__ pressure room.

11. The onset of myoglobin release is __1__ hour(s).

12. __eosinophils__ are a type of leukocyte that assist in engulfing antigen-antibody complexes during an allergic response.

13. The approximate range for PT is typically __10__ to __14__ seconds.

14. The normal range for magnesium (Mg2+) is typically __1.5__ to __2.5__.

15. The normal fasting blood glucose range is typically between __70__ to __100__.

16. Before a patient goes in for an operation, the __surgeon__ is responsible for explaining the surgical procedure and obtaining an informed consent.

17. The 6 categories in the Braden Scale include: __sensory__, __moisture__, __activity__, __mobility__, __nutrition__, and __friction & shear__

18. A medical order for the use of restraints must be obtained within __1__ minute(s)/ ~~hour(s)~~/day(s).

19. The "C" in the RACE acronym for remembering the proper order of actions to be initiated in the event of a fire emergency stands for __Confin__.

20. Generally, a 3/8 or 5/8 inch needle would be used for a __Sub Q__ injection.

Check your answers on page 140

6

WEEK 1 ACTIVITIES

2. Fill in the Picmonic: Normal Electrolyte Lab Values

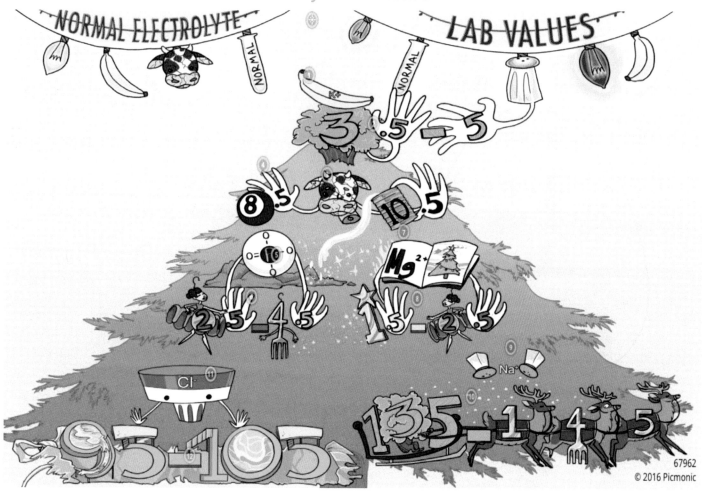

1. K+ ₃.₅₋₅

2. 3.5~5

3. Ca

4. 8.5-10.5

5. phosphate

6. 2.5-4.5

7. mg

8. 1.5-2.5

9. Na

10. 135~145

11. Cl

12. 95-105

notes:

3. Question of the Day:

A 19-year-old female patient arrives in the emergency department after she took a handful of oxycodone pills. She is unconscious and breathing at a rate of 7 breaths per minute. Which acid-base imbalance is the patient at highest risk of developing?

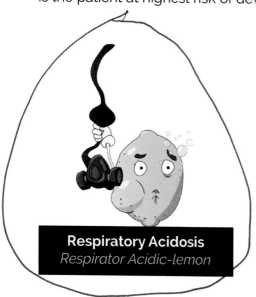

Respiratory Acidosis
Respirator Acidic-lemon

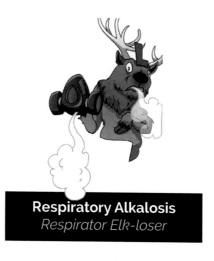

Respiratory Alkalosis
Respirator Elk-loser

Metabolic Alkalosis
Metal-ball Elk-loser

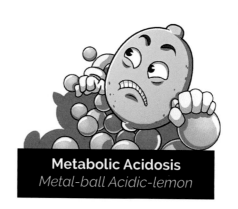

Metabolic Acidosis
Metal-ball Acidic-lemon

Check your answers
on page 140

4. Match the Lung Sounds!

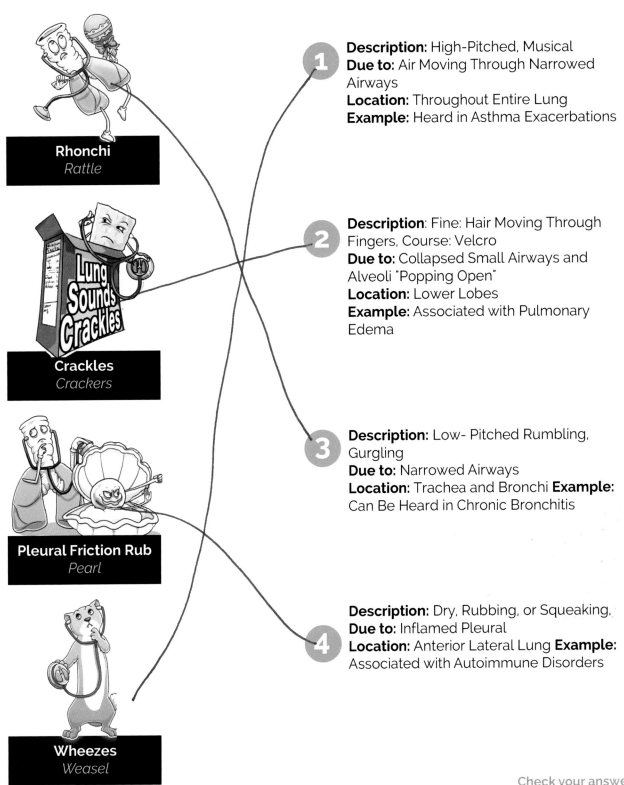

Rhonchi
Rattle

Crackles
Crackers

Pleural Friction Rub
Pearl

Wheezes
Weasel

1 **Description:** High-Pitched, Musical
Due to: Air Moving Through Narrowed Airways
Location: Throughout Entire Lung
Example: Heard in Asthma Exacerbations

2 **Description:** Fine: Hair Moving Through Fingers, Course: Velcro
Due to: Collapsed Small Airways and Alveoli "Popping Open"
Location: Lower Lobes
Example: Associated with Pulmonary Edema

3 **Description:** Low- Pitched Rumbling, Gurgling
Due to: Narrowed Airways
Location: Trachea and Bronchi **Example:** Can Be Heard in Chronic Bronchitis

4 **Description:** Dry, Rubbing, or Squeaking,
Due to: Inflamed Pleural
Location: Anterior Lateral Lung **Example:** Associated with Autoimmune Disorders

Check your answers on page 140

5. Fill in the Picmonic: Right Heart Failure Assessment

1. JVD
2. Peripheral edema
3. ~~BUG~~ HepatoSplenomegaly
4. Nocturia
5. weight gain
6. ascites
7. fatigue

notes:

6. Fill in the Picmonic: Left Heart Failure Assessment

1. pulmonary Congestion
2. Pink frothy Sputum
3. wheezing or Crackles
4. dyspnea with exertion
5. Cough
6. fatigue
7. tachycardia
8. weak peripheral pulse
9. S3, S4 heart sounds

notes:

WEEK 2

Dates: _____

MY GOAL THIS WEEK IS TO DO ____ PRACTICE QUESTIONS

WORDS OF INSPIRATION:

"The best way to find yourself is to lose yourself in the service of others."

- Mahatma Ghandi

THINGS I NEED TO WORK ON:

1. _____
2. _____
3. _____
4. _____
5. _____

ADVICE: When you miss a question (and you will, hotpants) make sure you take the time to review why you missed it; quickly. Then review the Picmonic on the topic to make sure you will remember it next time!

DAY 8 ☐

TODAY'S FOCUS

6am	
7am	
8am	
9am	
10am	
11am	
12pm	
1pm	
2pm	
3pm	
4pm	
5pm	
6pm	
7pm	
8pm	
9pm	
10pm	
11pm	
12am	

PATHWAY: Endocrine System > Assessments
11 PICMONICS: 55MINS
☐ Endocrine Glands (11)

> Disorders
31 PICMONICS: 2HRS 35MINS
☐ Hypothalamic & Pituitary Disorders (4)
☐ Thyroid Disorders (7)
☐ Parathyroid Disorders (2)
☐ Diabetes (6)
☐ Mineral & Bone Disorders (7)
☐ Adrenal Disorders (5)

DAY 9 ☐

TODAY'S FOCUS

6am	
7am	
8am	
9am	
10am	
11am	
12pm	
1pm	
2pm	
3pm	
4pm	
5pm	
6pm	
7pm	
8pm	
9pm	
10pm	
11pm	
12am	

PATHWAY: Endocrine System > Pharmacology
13 PICMONICS: 1HR 5MINS
☐ Diabetic Medications (11)
☐ Thyroid Medications (2)

Webinar:
☐ Endocrine System Made Easy

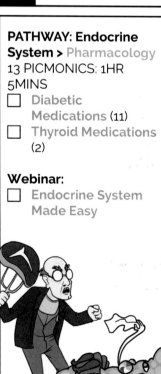

DAY 10 ☐

TODAY'S FOCUS

6am	
7am	
8am	
9am	
10am	
11am	
12pm	
1pm	
2pm	
3pm	
4pm	
5pm	
6pm	
7pm	
8pm	
9pm	
10pm	
11pm	
12am	

PATHWAY: Gastrointestinal System > Nursing Basics
40 PICMONICS: 3HRS 20MINS
☐ Oral & Esophageal Disorders (5)
☐ Stomach Disorders (5)
☐ Noninflammatory Intestinal Disorders (9)
☐ Inflammatory Intestinal Disorders (6)
☐ Liver Disorders (6)
☐ Biliary Disorders (3)
☐ Pancreatic Disorders (4)
☐ Malnutrition & Obesity (2)

DAY 11

TODAY'S FOCUS

6am	
7am	
8am	
9am	
10am	
11am	
12pm	
1pm	
2pm	
3pm	
4pm	
5pm	
6pm	
7pm	
8pm	
9pm	
10pm	
11pm	
12am	

DAY 12

TODAY'S FOCUS

6am	
7am	
8am	
9am	
10am	
11am	
12pm	
1pm	
2pm	
3pm	
4pm	
5pm	
6pm	
7pm	
8pm	
9pm	
10pm	
11pm	
12am	

DAY 13

TODAY'S FOCUS

6am	
7am	
8am	
9am	
10am	
11am	
12pm	
1pm	
2pm	
3pm	
4pm	
5pm	
6pm	
7pm	
8pm	
9pm	
10pm	
11pm	
12am	

DAY14

TODAY'S FOCUS

6am	
7am	
8am	
9am	
10am	
11am	
12pm	
1pm	
2pm	
3pm	
4pm	
5pm	
6pm	
7pm	
8pm	
9pm	
10pm	
11pm	
12am	

PATHWAY: Gastrointestinal System
> Pharmacology
18 PICMONICS: 1HR 30MINS
☐ Vitamins & Minerals (12)
☐ Gastrointestinal Pharmacology (6)

Webinars:
☐ The Gastrointestinal System

PATHWAY: Hematologic System > Assessments
40 PICMONICS: 2HRS 20MINS
☐ Blood Physiology (5)
☐ *Lab Values (32)
☐ Bleeding Precautions (3)

*NOTE: You can skip this path if you've already mastered the Lab Values Picmonics on Day 1, or you can use it as a review!

PATHWAY: Hematologic System > Disorders
21 PICMONICS: 1HR 45MINS
☐ Anemias (2)
☐ Blood Transfusions (4)
☐ *Shock & Sepsis (3)
☐ Leukemias & Lymphomas (5)
☐ Other Hematological Disorders (7)

> Pharmacology
8 PICMONICS: 40MINS
☐ Anticoagulants (8)

*NOTE: You can skip this path if you've already mastered the Shock & Sepsis Picmonics on Day 6, or you can use it as a review!

PATHWAY: Musculoskeletal System
> Assessments
8 PICMONICS: 40MINS
☐ Fractures & Surgery (8)

> DISORDERS
18 PICMONICS: 1HR 30MINS
☐ Musculoskeletal Trauma (5)
☐ Musculoskeletal Disorders (13)

> Pharmacology
10 PICMONICS: 50MINS
☐ Anti-inflammatories (9)
☐ Other Musculoskeletal Pharmacology (1)

1. For each insulin, fill in the onset of action, and duration of action!

RAPID-ACTING:		
RAPID		**Insulin Lispro (Humalog):** Onset: Duration:
		Insulin Aspart (Novolog): Onset: Duration:
		Insulin Glulisine (Apidra): Onset: Duration:
SHORT-ACTING:		
SHORT		**Regular Insulin (Humalin R):** Onset: Duration:
INTERMEDIATE ACTING:		
INTERMEDIATE		**Isophane NPH (Humalin N):** Onset: Duration:
LONG-ACTING:		
LONG		**Detemir (Levemir):** Onset: Duration:
		Glargine (Lantus): Onset: Duration:

Check your answers
on page 140

WEEK 2 ACTIVITIES

2. Fill in the Picmonic: Crohn's Disease Assessment

1. _____
2. _____
3. _____
4. _____
5. _____
6. _____
7. _____
8. _____
9. _____

notes:

3. Fill in the Picmonic: Ulcerative Colitis

1. _____
2. _____
3. _____
4. _____
5. _____
6. _____

notes:

WEEK 2 ACTIVITIES

4. List 3 Differences Between Heparin and Warfarin

VS

Heparin *Hippie-heron*	**Warfarin** *War-fairy*
Safe for pregnancy? (Yes/No)	**Safe for pregnancy?** (Yes/No)
Antidote:	**Antidote:**
Monitoring lab test:	**Monitoring lab test:**
Nursing considerations:	**Nursing considerations:**

Check your answers on page 140

5. Question of the Day:

An 80-year-old female patient with an intestinal blockage is ordered total parenteral nutrition (TPN). The student nurse assigned to her is learning about TPN preparation and administration. Which statement made by the student nurse indicates the need for further education?

1. "I will not increase the rate of TPN if the infusion falls behind schedule."
2. "I will administer this solution slowly."
3. "I will administer this solution through a large central vein."
4. "I will add the patient's other medications to this solution."
5. "I will use an IV fi ter with the TPN solution."

6. Question of the Day:

You are taking your friend to a cocktail party. She knows you are a nurse and tells you that every time she takes her cholesterol medication she turns "red as a beet." She's worried this is serious and asks you what she should do. What medication is she most likely taking?

Atropine
@-trooper

Vancomycin
Van-tank-mice

Niacin
Nice-sun

Cholestyramine
Coal-star-man

Check your answers
on page 141

7. Crossword Puzzle: All Things Blood

Check your answers
on page 141

Across

3. This is a term that is used for an individual who can donate blood to individuals of any group.

4. Individuals with this type of blood have the B antigen on the surface of their RBCs and blood serum containing IgM antibodies.

5. This is a term that is used for an individual who can receive blood from any group.

7. This type of blood product is used for severe anemia or in situations of acute blood loss.

8. This is a protein found on the covering of red blood cells.

9. This type of transfusion reaction usually develops within the first 15 minutes of a blood transfusion.

10. This type of blood product contains red blood cells, white blood cells, and platelets in plasma.

Down

1. This describes the liquid portion of whole blood, minus the blood cells, and is rich in clotting factors and proteins.

2. This is special tubing that is used when administering blood products.

6. This type of blood product is used to treat bleeding caused by thrombocytopenia.

19

WEEK 3

Dates: _____

MY GOAL THIS WEEK IS TO DO ____ PRACTICE QUESTIONS

WORDS OF INSPIRATION:

"Nurses dispense comfort, compassion, and caring without even a prescription."

- Val Saintsbury

THINGS I NEED TO WORK ON:
1. _____
2. _____
3. _____
4. _____
5. _____

ADVICE: Our users self-report the most success in retention after using a Picmonic 3-5 times. So, make sure you review a specific topic as you study.

DAY 15 ☐

TODAY'S FOCUS

6am	
7am	
8am	
9am	
10am	
11am	
12pm	
1pm	
2pm	
3pm	
4pm	
5pm	
6pm	
7pm	
8pm	
9pm	
10pm	
11pm	
12am	

PATHWAY: Integumentary System
> Disorders
15 PICMONICS: 1HR 15MINS
☐ Skin Cancer (2)
☐ Burns (7)
☐ Skin Breakdown & Wounds (6)

> Pharmacology
9 PICMONICS: 45MINS
☐ Integumentary Pharmacology (9)

DAY 16 ☐

TODAY'S FOCUS

6am	
7am	
8am	
9am	
10am	
11am	
12pm	
1pm	
2pm	
3pm	
4pm	
5pm	
6pm	
7pm	
8pm	
9pm	
10pm	
11pm	
12am	

PATHWAY: Nervous System > Disorders
36 PICMONICS: 3HRs
☐ Central Nervous System Disorders (9)
☐ Peripheral Nervous System Disorders (5)
☐ Seizures (3)
☐ Stroke & Traumatic Brain Injury (8)
☐ Infectious Disease (3)
☐ Eye Disorders (5)
☐ Ear Disorders (3)

DAY 17 ☐

TODAY'S FOCUS

6am	
7am	
8am	
9am	
10am	
11am	
12pm	
1pm	
2pm	
3pm	
4pm	
5pm	
6pm	
7pm	
8pm	
9pm	
10pm	
11pm	
12am	

PATHWAY: Nervous System > Pharmacology > Autonomic Pharm
17 PICMONICS: 1HR 25MINS
☐ Adrenergics (8)
☐ Cholinergics (9)

> Pharmacology> Other Nervous System Pharm
26 PICMONICS: 2HR 10MINS
☐ Anesthetics (4)
☐ Antiepileptics (8)
☐ Other Nervous System Pharm (14)

Webinar:
☐ Nervous System

TODAY'S FOCUS	TODAY'S FOCUS	TODAY'S FOCUS	TODAY'S FOCUS

Time	Day 18	Day 19	Day 20	Day 21
6am				
7am				
8am				
9am				
10am				
11am				
12pm				
1pm				
2pm				
3pm				
4pm				
5pm				
6pm				
7pm				
8pm				
9pm				
10pm				
11pm				
12am				

PATHWAY: Immune System & Oncology

> Immune System > Disorders
6 PICMONICS: 30MINS
☐ Immune Disorders (6)

> Immune System > Pharmacology
9 PICMONICS: 45MINS
☐ Immunosuppresants (6)

> Oncology > Disorders
19 PICMONICS: 1HR 35MINS

☐ Cancer Assessments (12)
☐ Leukemias and Lymphomas (12)
☐ Other Tumors and Cancers (12)

> Oncology > Disorders
5 PICMONICS: 25MINS
☐ Antineoplastic Medications (5)

PATHWAY: Genitourinary/Renal System > Disorders
15 PICMONICS: 1HR 55MINS
☐ Urinary Disorders (4)
☐ Renal Disorders (9)
☐ Kidney Injury & Chronic Kidney Disease (4)

> Pharmacology
7 PICMONICS: 35 MINS
☐ Diuretics (6)
☐ Other Renal Pharmacology (1)

Webinar:
☐ Renal Concepts and Pharmacology

PATHWAY: Reproductive System

> Disorders
20 PICMONICS: 1HR 40MINS
☐ Male Reproductive Disorders (7)
☐ Female Reproductive Disorders (7)
☐ Breast Disorders (2)
☐ Sexually Transmitted Infections (5)

> Pharmacology
7 PICMONICS: 35 MINS
☐ Reproductive Pharmacology (7)

PATHWAY: Infectious Disease > Disorders
5 PICMONICS: 25MINS
☐ Sexually Transmitted Infections (5)

> Pharmacology
23 PICMONICS: 1HR 55MINS
☐ Antibiotics (19)
☐ Antivirals (4)

1. Fill in the Blank

1. According to the "Rule of Nines," the anterior torso, including the chest, accounts for ____% TBSA.

2. According to the "Rule of Nines," the posterior of each leg accounts for ____% TBSA.

3. The Parkland formula is used to calculate the amount of fluid given to a burn patient in the first ____ minutes/hour(s).

4. The "C" in the acronym RICE, for interventions to provide first-aid treatment for soft tissue injuries, stands for _____.

5. _____ exudate consists of leukocytes and blood resulting in a light pink watery fluid. This type of fluid can also be seen in early stages of healing, and the amount should decrease as healing progresses.

6. _____ are a class of drugs often used to control seizures because of their anticonvulsant properties.

7. Patients experiencing a seizure ____ (should/should not) be restrained.

8. Parkinson's disease is characterized by a decreased production of _____ by the substantia nigra in the brain.

9. The 5 A's of Alzheimer's are _____, _____, _____, _____, _____.

10. Ischemic strokes are classified in to two types: _____ and _____.

Check your answers
on page 141

2. Question of the Day

A 23-year-old male patient is in the clinic presenting with painful blisters around his genitals. He is diagnosed with genital herpes, and he is confused and worried as to what this means. He asks the nurse for more information. Which statements does the nurse include when educating the patient? Select all that apply:

1. "Patients are not infectious during recurrences of this infection."

2. "Recurrences of this infection may be triggered by stress."

3. "Prodromal symptoms include tingling, burning and itching at the site where lesions typically reappear."

4. "A characteristic of this virus is the presence of painless chancres."

5. "Penicillin is often given as a treatment for this virus."

Check your answers
on page 141

WEEK 3 ACTIVITIES

3. Fill in the Picmonic: Left Hemisphere Stroke Assessment

1. _____
2. _____
3. _____
4. _____
5. _____
6. _____
7. _____
8.

notes:

4. Fill in the Picmonic: Right Hemisphere Stroke Assessment

1. _____
2. _____
3. _____
4. _____
5. _____
6. _____
7. _____
8.

notes:

5. Word Search: Meningitis

```
M V H C B X N T K A I H H F N
S E I Z U R E S M K B W J L Y
I V G S L P C N V U E M S H R
K X H N G Y D S B K G M U L Q
V N P I I C L W R X O F D N U
F Z I N N T S F B N G C B W Q
S I T I G N I N E M C W A J L
L Q C Q F K P M P W M F L O E
B U H Z O J A E O D H Z H H H
O F E P N L E N K V Y D C U Q
J Q D B T P U R P U R A T S V
N U C H A L R I G I D I T Y T
W U R O N A U S E A I L R I U
S W Y W E A V H E M U A R Z K
X G W J L L O H L N S S M H D
```

1. Meningitis
2. Nausea
3. Vomiting
4. Nuchal Rigidity
5. Headache
6. Purpura
7. Seizures
8. Opisthotonus Position
9. High-Pitched Cry
10. Bulging Fontanel

6. Question of the Day

A 70-year-old female patient is in the hospital in a hypokalemic state from diuretic use. Prior to discharge, the nurse is giving the patient diet education. Which of the following foods would be best to recommend including in her diet? Select all that apply:

1. Avocados
2. Spinach
3. Potatoes
4. White Rice
5. Strawberries
6. Peanut Butter

Check your answers on page 141

7. Match the Antibiotic with Possible Side Effects:

Fluoroquinolones
Flower-queen

Tetracyclines
Tetris-cycle

Macrolides
Macaroni-lights

Vancomycin
Van-tank-mice

Cephalosporins
Chef-spore-head

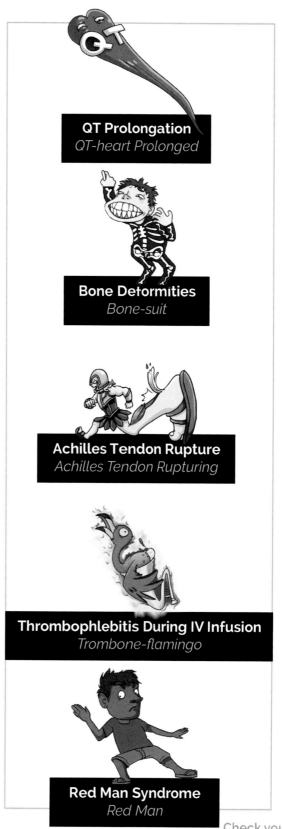

QT Prolongation
QT-heart Prolonged

Bone Deformities
Bone-suit

Achilles Tendon Rupture
Achilles Tendon Rupturing

Thrombophlebitis During IV Infusion
Trombone-flamingo

Red Man Syndrome
Red Man

Check your answers
on page 141

WEEK 4

Dates: _____

MY GOAL THIS WEEK IS TO DO ____ PRACTICE QUESTIONS

THINGS I NEED TO WORK ON:
1. _____
2. _____
3. _____
4. _____
5. _____

DAY 22

TODAY'S FOCUS

6am, 7am, 8am, 9am, 10am, 11am, 12pm, 1pm, 2pm, 3pm, 4pm, 5pm, 6pm, 7pm, 8pm, 9pm, 10pm, 11pm, 12am

PATHWAY: Obstetrics >
Reproductive Cycle
5 PICMONICS: 25MINS
- ☐ Fetal Circulation (3)
- ☐ Menstrual Cycle (2)

> Prenatal Period
18 PICMONICS: 1HR 30MINS
- ☐ Prenatal Period (8)
- ☐ Discomforts of Pregnancy (3)
- ☐ Signs of Pregnancy (3)
- ☐ Diagnostics Tests (4)

> Labor & Delivery
13 PICMONICS: 1HR 5MINS
- ☐ Labor & Delivery (7)
- ☐ Neonatal Assessments (3)

DAY 23

TODAY'S FOCUS

6am, 7am, 8am, 9am, 10am, 11am, 12pm, 1pm, 2pm, 3pm, 4pm, 5pm, 6pm, 7pm, 8pm, 9pm, 10pm, 11pm, 12am

PATHWAY: Obstetrics
> Pregnancy Complications
23 PICMONICS: 1HR 55MINS
- ☐ Pregnancy Complications (11)
- ☐ Medical Complications (8)
- ☐ Implantation Abnormalities (4)

> TORCH Infections
5 PICMONICS: 25MINS
- ☐ TORCH Infections (5)

> Postpartum Period
5 PICMONICS: 25MINS
- ☐ Postpartum Period (5)

DAY 24

TODAY'S FOCUS

6am, 7am, 8am, 9am, 10am, 11am, 12pm, 1pm, 2pm, 3pm, 4pm, 5pm, 6pm, 7pm, 8pm, 9pm, 10pm, 11pm, 12am

PATHWAY: Pediatric Nursing > Assessments
15 PICMONICS: 1HR 15MINS
- ☐ Early Developmental Milestones (10)
- ☐ Pediatric Vaccination Schedules (5)

> Pediatric Disorders
22 PICMONICS: 2HR 50MINS
- ☐ Congenital Abnormalities (7)
- ☐ Cardiac Abnormalities (2)
- ☐ TORCH Infections (5)
- ☐ Other Pediatric Disorders (8)

6am	
7am	
8am	
9am	
10am	
11am	
12pm	
1pm	
2pm	
3pm	
4pm	
5pm	
6pm	
7pm	
8pm	
9pm	
10pm	
11pm	
12am	

TODAY'S FOCUS

PATHWAY: Pediatric Nursing > Infectious Disease
17 PICMONICS: 1HR 25MINS
☐ Childhood Viral Exanthems (6)
☐ Other Childhood Infections (11)

6am	
7am	
8am	
9am	
10am	
11am	
12pm	
1pm	
2pm	
3pm	
4pm	
5pm	
6pm	
7pm	
8pm	
9pm	
10pm	
11pm	
12am	

TODAY'S FOCUS

PATHWAY: Psychiatric > Psychiatric Disorders
33 PICMONICS: 2HRS 45MINS
☐ Anxiety Disorders (3)
☐ Mood Disorders (9)
☐ Cognitive Disorders (5)
☐ Personality Disorders (11)
☐ Eating Disorders (3)
☐ Pediatric Psychiatric Disorders (2)

6am	
7am	
8am	
9am	
10am	
11am	
12pm	
1pm	
2pm	
3pm	
4pm	
5pm	
6pm	
7pm	
8pm	
9pm	
10pm	
11pm	
12am	

TODAY'S FOCUS

PATHWAY: Psychiatric > Substance Related
10 PICMONICS: 50MINS
☐ Substance Related Disorders (10)

6am	
7am	
8am	
9am	
10am	
11am	
12pm	
1pm	
2pm	
3pm	
4pm	
5pm	
6pm	
7pm	
8pm	
9pm	
10pm	
11pm	
12am	

TODAY'S FOCUS

PATHWAY: Psychiatric > Psychiatric Pharmacology
32 PICMONICS: 2HRS 40MINS
☐ Anxiolytics & Hypnotics (5)
☐ Antipsychotics (12)
☐ Antidepressants (10)
☐ CNS Stimulants (5)

Webinar:
☐ Everything Psychiatric

1. Fill in the Blank

1. Chadwick's sign is considered a _____ sign of pregnancy.

2. Quickening is considered a _____ sign of pregnancy.

3. The neonate is assessed using this APGAR score at intervals of _____ and _____ minutes after birth.

4. A neonate with an APGAR score of 6 would indicate_____.

5. The "EL" in the acronym for HELLP syndrome stands for _____.

6. A pregnant woman should be placed in _____ position as an intervention for preeclampsia.

7. Assessment findings for this implantation abnormality includes painless, bright red vaginal bleeding: _____.

8. By this age, stranger anxiety typically begins to develop: _____.

9. By this age, the Babinski reflex, also known as the plantar reflex, typically disappears: _____.

10. _____ is an intestinal obstruction in children with assessment findings that include episodic abdominal pain, a sausage-shaped mass, and red currant jelly stools.

Check your answers
on page 142

2. Match the Psychiatric Disorder to the appropriate description

Obsessive Compulsive Disorder
OCD-tiles

Schizophrenia
Sketchy-fern

Post Traumatic Stress Disorder
Post Trauma-spike

Bipolar Disorder
Bi-polar-bear

Hallucinations
Halloween

Delusions
Doll-illusionist

Borderline Personality Disorder
Borderlined Person

Illusions
Illusionary-stairs

Antisocial Personality Disorder
Ant-tie-social-book

1 Disregards the rights of others, often manipulative and lacks remorse for actions

2 Has chronic feelings of emptiness, poor self-image, self-destructive behaviors and is unable to maintain stable relationships

3 Anxiety about losing control, has repetitive, intrusive thoughts that interfere with daily functioning

4 When manic, has nonstop physical activity, rapid speech, flight of ideas, and euphoric mood

5 No external stimulus

6 A fixed, false belief

7 Re-experiences traumatic events, is avoidant, and has self-destructive behaviors

8 Misinterpretation of stimulus

9 Has flat affect, hallucinations or delusions, illogical thinking, impaired judgment or memory

Check your answers on page 142

3. Question of the Day

You are on an acute care psych unit when a 25-year-old woman is brought in by her mother, who tells you she has been acting "strange." She explained that she had purchased $2,500 worth of coffee mugs last week, cannot sleep, and is destined to complete a thesis on world peace by working day and night. The patient is started on lithium. Which of the following statements by the patient indicates a need for further education? Select all that apply:

1. I will take my birth control routinely.

2. If I miss a dose of this medication I should double up the next dose.

3. Because this medication works on my Serotonin receptors, I will be sure to let my doctor know if there is an increase or decrease in blood pressure and check it weekly.

4. This medication may cause thyroid problems.

Check your answers
on page 142

4. Fill in the Picmonic: Amniocentesis

1. _____
2. _____
3. _____
4. _____
5. _____
6. _____
7. _____
8.

notes:

5. Fill in the Picmonic: Benzodiazepine Intoxication Assessment

1. _____
2. _____
3. _____
4. _____
5. _____
6. _____
7. _____
8. _____

notes:

6. Crossword Puzzle: Need To Know Pharmacology

Across

7. This may be a side effect of glucocorticoids.

9. The reversal agent to heparin.

10. Wine and aged cheese are contraindicated when taking this class of drugs (abv).

Down

1. Glucagon is the reversal agent to this drug category.

2. A side effect of NSAIDs.

3. This medication is often indicated for preterm labor contractions.

4. This is a common fatal side effect of the drug clozapine.

5. This anticoagulant is contraindicated in pregnancy.

6. Neuroleptic malignant syndrome is a life-threatening complication associated with these types of drugs.

8. Glargine (Lantus) is _____ acting.

Check your answers
on page 142

Don't have time to review all of the Picmonics?
Although we don't recommend skipping, if it must happen, don't skip these top 100!

Get the playlist by scanning this QR Code!

FUNDAMENTALS: BEGINNING

🄗 You can only skip ahead in the nursing process in a few scenarios. The main one: If I don't do something now.... This patient will be in immediate danger or face serious health threats. Don't kill your patients! Example: Your patient is cyanotic and in obvious respiratory distress. Do you continue to assess? Nope. You sit them up, give them oxygen, etc. BUT; As a general rule: Skipping ahead in the nursing process is the wrong answer.

🄗 Be sure to know which patients you would put together in the same room.

- ☐ The Nursing Process
- ☐ Maslow's Hierarchy of Needs
- ☐ Contact Precautions
- ☐ Standard Precautions
- ☐ Droplet-Airborne Precautions

FUNDAMENTALS: LAB VALUES

🄗 You are most likely to see Potassium, Sodium, Magnesium, Calcium, Chloride, HgB, PT/ INR, and pH lab values.

- ☐ Normal Electrolyte Lab Values
- ☐ WBC Differential Lab Value
- ☐ Hemoglobin (Hgb Lab Value
- ☐ pH Blood and Urine Lab Value

FUNDAMENTALS: HOSPITAL CARE & MEDICATION ADMINISTRATION

🄗 Safe medication administration techniques is a must-know.
- ☐ Aseptic Technique
- ☐ IM Medication Administration
- ☐ 6 Rights of Medication Administration

FUNDAMENTALS: PHYSICAL EXAM

🄗 For MRI's; no metal objects, no pacemakers, safe during pregnancy.

- ☐ Vital Signs - Adult
- ☐ Glasgow Coma Scale
- ☐ Tuberculosis Skin Mantoux Test (PPD)
- ☐ Magnetic Resonance Imaging (MRI)

FUNDAMENTALS: COMMUNICATION & CULTURE

🄗 Important: Know your patients cultural dietary restrictions.

🄗 Remember you can only delegate stable patients, and only an RN can do patient assessments, interpretations, or evaluations.

- ☐ Religion & Dietary Preferences Overview
- ☐ 5 Rights of Delegation

MED-SURG: FLUIDS & ELECTROLYTES

🄗 These questions are common. If you have to guess here, a common answer is arrhythmia.

- ☐ Hypokalemia
- ☐ Hyperkalemia
- ☐ Hyponatremia
- ☐ Hypernatremia

PENCIL VILLAIN'S TOP 100 PICMONICS FOR NCLEX®

MED-SURG: RESPIRATORY DISORDERS

🄗 Airway. Airway. Airway. Be sure to know how a patient in respiratory distress will present during an assessment. Also be sure to choose the basic interventions before the more difficult ones.

- [ ] COPD Overview (Chronic Obstructive Pulmonary Disease Overview
- [ ] Asthma Implementation and Education
- [ ] Tuberculosis Assessment

MED-SURG: GENITOURINARY, RENAL DISORDERS & DIURETICS

🄗 Be watchful of the older patient with a fever and confusion! They are likely to have a urinary tract infection. Females and patients with indwelling catheters are even higher risk

🄗 You can learn a lot about someone from their urine. Keep in mind patients with decreased kidney function are not able to remove toxins as well as many drugs from their bodies.

🄗 HCTZ is often given to African American patients for hypertension. Another common reminder is that loops lose calcium.

- [ ] UTI Symptoms
- [ ] Chronic Kidney Disease Interventions
- [ ] Loop Diuretics
- [ ] Hydrochlorothiazide HCTZ

MED-SURG: CARDIOVASCULAR DISORDERS

🄗 These are a few Picmonics you should not skip over. Know that LEFT heart failure fluid backs up into the LUNGS and that RIGHT heart failure fluid backs up into the BODY. Make sure you also know the difference between unstable and stable angina.

- [ ] Hypertension Intervention
- [ ] Stable Angina
- [ ] Unstable Angina
- [ ] Heart Failure Interventions

MED-SURG: CARDIOVASCULAR PHARMACOLOGY

🄗 Be sure to remember which drug requires which lab monitoring. With heparin you must monitor PT/PTT and with warfarin you monitor PT/INR.

🄗 There are several medications that have narrow therapeutic ranges, meaning they have a higher risk for toxicity. Test makers love them.

- [ ] Aspirin (Acetylsalicylic Acid)
- [ ] Heparin (Unfractionated)
- [ ] Warfarin (Coumadin)
- [ ] Hypertension Medications

MED-SURG: ENDOCRINE AND METABOLIC DISORDERS

🄗 You must be able to distinguish the assessment findings in hypothyroidism versus hyperthyroidism.

🄗 Know the different types of diabetes and the early presentations of each.

- [ ] Hypothyroidism Assessment
- [ ] Hypoglycemia Assessment
- [ ] Hypoglycemia Intervention
- [ ] Diabetes Assessment

MED-SURG: ENDOCRINE PHARMACOLOGY

- [ ] Levothyroxine (Synthroid) Insulin
- [ ] Metformin (Glucophage)

MED-SURG: GI DISORDERS

Ⓗ Be sure to know the assessment and interventions for GERD.

Ⓗ Knowing how each type of hepatitis is transmitted is important.

☐ Gastroesophageal Reflux Disease (GERD) Assessment
☐ Acute Pancreatitis Assessment
☐ Hepatitis B (HBV) Assessment
☐ Cirrhosis Assessment

MED-SURG: NEUROLOGICAL DISORDERS

Ⓗ Don't skip over Parkinson's, Alzheimer's and delirium; you are likely to see questions related to these and have to distinguish between them.

☐ Seizure Precautions
☐ Increased Intracranial Pressure (ICP) Interventions
☐ Parkinson's Disease Assessment
☐ Alzheimer's Disease Assessment (Early Symptoms)

MED-SURG: NEUROLOGICAL PHARMACOLOGY

Ⓗ Know the side effects of these important medications.
☐ Morphine
☐ Naloxone (Narcan)
☐ Benztropine (Cogentin)
☐ Phenytoin (Dilantin)

MED-SURG: HEMATOLOGICAL AND ONCOLOGICAL DISORDERS

Ⓗ You are likely to get a question about one of these types of cancers. Be sure to know the warning signs and screening tests for each.

☐ Venous Thromboembolism (DVT) Assessment
☐ Venous Thromboembolism (DVT) Interventions
☐ Breast Cancer Diagnosis
☐ Prostate Cancer Assessment

MED-SURG: AUTOIMMUNE, MUSCULOSKELETAL DISORDERS, & ANTI-INFLAMMATORIES

Ⓗ Know the key differences to differentiate osteoarthritis from rheumatoid arthritis. Don't forget the patients at risk for osteoporosis (like: postmenopausal women, and patients taking corticosteroids)

Ⓗ Prednisone is a common steroid medication. Know the important side effects and subsequent patient education

☐ Rheumatoid Arthritis Assessment
☐ Osteoporosis Assessment
☐ Compartment Syndrome Assessment
☐ Ibuprofen (Advil, Motrin)
☐ Prednisone (Glucocorticoids)

MED-SURG: PERIOPERATIVE CARE

Ⓗ Know whose responsibility it is to get informed consent!

Ⓗ Know when a chest tube isn't working properly.

☐ Preoperative Care
☐ Chest Tubes: Management and Care

MED-SURG: BURNS & SKIN INTEGRITY

Ⓗ Make sure you know what to do to prevent pressure ulcer formation.

☐ Burns Interventions
☐ Braden Scale
☐ Interventions for Impaired Skin Integrity

MED-SURG: ANTIBIOTICS

🅗 You should be comfortable knowing the main side effects with each antibiotic class. Spend a little more time knowing the side effects and patient education rather than which infection we give them for.

- [ ] Penicillin
- [ ] Cephalosporins
- [ ] Vancomycin
- [ ] Tetracyclines Overview

OBSTETRICS: PREGNANCY COMPLICATIONS

🅗 Don't skip over RhoGAM; you need to know the times to administer it.

- [ ] Preeclampsia Assessment
- [ ] Severe Preeclampsia
- [ ] Eclampsia
- [ ] RhoGam [Rho(D) Immune Globulin]

OBSTETRICS: LABOR & DELIVERY, POSTPARTUM

🅗 We'd be surprised if you don't get a question on decelerations and accelerations. VEAL CHOP is your best friend.

🅗 Magnesium basically slows muscle contraction. You can find the signs and symptoms under the hypermagnesemia picmonic. (Ps: It's decreased DTR's, and you should slow the rate of the medication and have the antidote ready: calcium gluconate)

- [ ] Decelerations (and Accelerations) Overview
- [ ] Magnesium Sulfate
- [ ] Oxytocin (Pitocin)
- [ ] Postpartum Nursing Assessment

PEDIATRICS: EARLY DEVELOPMENTAL MILESTONES

🅗 It is very likely that one of your OB questions will ask you to calculate an APGAR score on a newborn at 1 or 5 minutes.

- [ ] APGAR SCORE
- [ ] Age 2 Months- Developmental Milestones
- [ ] Age 6 Months- Developmental Milestones
- [ ] Age 9 Months- Developmental Milestones
- [ ] Age 1 Year- Developmental Milestones

PEDIATRICS: DISORDERS & INFECTIOUS DISEASES

- [ ] Respiratory Syncytial Virus (RSV) Assessment
- [ ] Tetralogy of Fallot

PSYCHIATRIC NURSING: PSYCH DISORDERS

🅗 Be very familiar with suicide risk factors and what to ask when assessing

🅗 Restraints should ONLY be used AS A LAST RESORT

- [ ] SIG E CAPS for Major Depressive Disorder (MDD)
- [ ] Schizophrenia Assessment
- [ ] Bipolar Disorder Assessment
- [ ] Suicide Assessment
- [ ] Use of Restraints

PSYCHIATRIC NURSING: PSYCH PHARMACOLOGY

- [ ] Benzodiazepine [Diazepam (Valium)]
- [ ] Fluoxetine (Prozac)
- [ ] Neuroleptic Malignant Syndrome
- [ ] Clozapine (Clozaril)

PSYCHIATRIC NURSING: SUBSTANCE ABUSE & TOXICITIES

🅗 You will likely be asked to identify and differentiate between patients who are alcoholic and abusing various drugs. Know the key differences in presentation.

🅗 Know your antidotes!

- [ ] Alcohol Abuse Interventions
- [ ] Opioid Abuse & Withdrawal Assessment
- [ ] Benzodiazepine Antidote

The Nursing Process

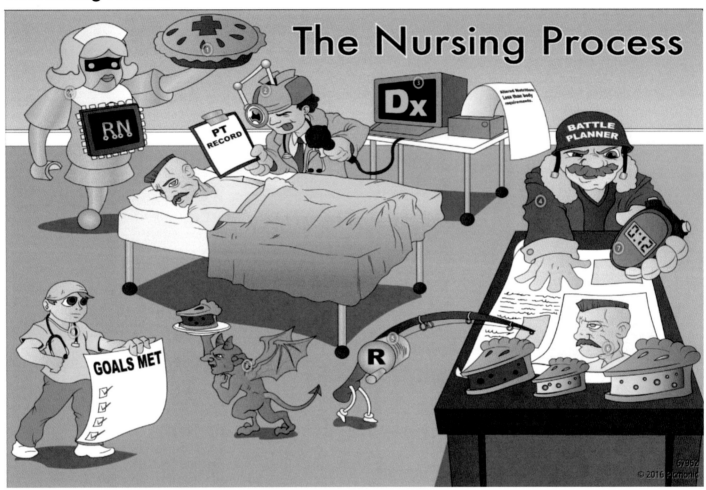

1. _____
2. _____
3. _____
4. _____
5. _____
6. _____
7. _____
8. _____
9. _____
   _____
   _____

notes:

Maslow's Hierarchy of Needs

1. _____
2. _____
3. _____
4. _____
5. _____
6. _____
7. _____
_____
_____
_____
_____

notes:

Contact Precautions

1. _____

2. _____

3. _____

4. _____

5. _____

6. _____

7. _____

8. _____

9. _____

10. _____

11. _____

notes:

Standard Precautions

67962
© 2016 Picmonic

1. _____

2. _____

3. _____

4. _____

5. _____

6. _____

7. _____

8. _____

9. _____

10. _____

11. _____

12. _____

notes:

Droplet-Airborne Precautions

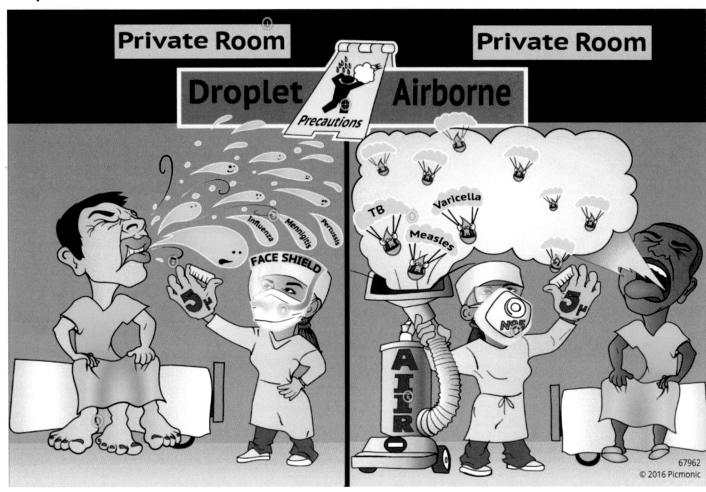

1. _____

2. _____

3. _____

4. _____

5. _____

6. _____

7. _____

8. _____

9. _____

_____

_____

notes:

WBC Differential Lab Value

1. _____
2. _____
3. _____
4. _____
5. _____
6. _____
7. _____
8. _____
9. _____

_____
_____

notes:

Normal Electrolyte Lab Values

© 2016 Picmonic
67962

1. _____
2. _____
3. _____
4. _____
5. _____
6. _____
7. _____
8. _____
9. _____
10. _____
11. _____
12.

notes:

pH - Blood and Urine Lab Value

67962
© 2016 Picmonic

1. _____
2. _____
3. _____
4. _____
_____
_____
_____
_____
_____
_____
_____

notes:

Hemoglobin (Hgb) Lab Values

1. _____
2. _____

_____

_____

_____

_____

_____

notes:

6 Rights of Medication Administration

1. _____

2. _____

3. _____

4. _____

5. _____

6. _____

7. _____

8. _____

9. _____

10. _____

_____

notes:

Aseptic Technique

1. _____
2. _____
3. _____
4. _____
5. _____
6. _____
7. _____
8. _____
9. _____
10. _____
11. _____

notes:

(IM) Intramuscular Medication Administration

1. _____
2. _____
3. _____
4. _____
5. _____
6. _____
7. _____
8. _____
9. _____
10. _____

notes:

Vital Signs - Adult

1. _____
2. _____
3. _____
4. _____
5. _____
6. _____
7. _____
8. _____
_____
_____
_____

notes:

Glasgow Coma Scale

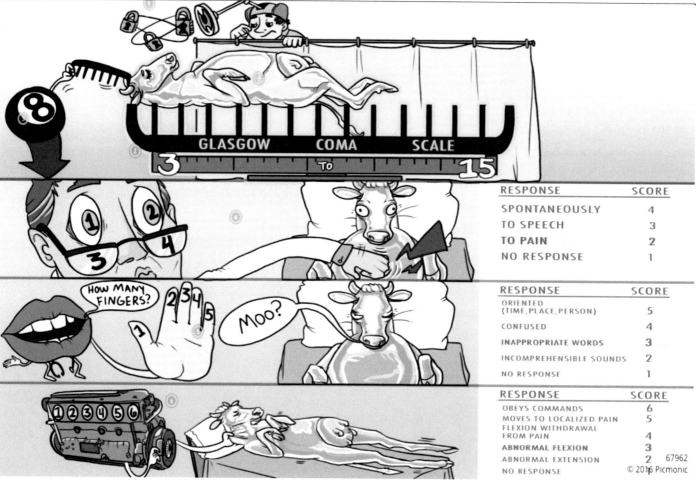

RESPONSE	SCORE
SPONTANEOUSLY	4
TO SPEECH	3
TO PAIN	2
NO RESPONSE	1

RESPONSE	SCORE
ORIENTED (TIME, PLACE, PERSON)	5
CONFUSED	4
INAPPROPRIATE WORDS	3
INCOMPREHENSIBLE SOUNDS	2
NO RESPONSE	1

RESPONSE	SCORE
OBEYS COMMANDS	6
MOVES TO LOCALIZED PAIN	5
FLEXION WITHDRAWAL FROM PAIN	4
ABNORMAL FLEXION	3
ABNORMAL EXTENSION	2
NO RESPONSE	

67962
© 2016 Picmonic

1. _____
2. _____
3. _____
4. _____
5. _____
6. _____
_____
_____
_____
_____
_____

notes:

Tuberculosis Skin Mantoux Test (PPD)

1. _____
2. _____
3. _____
4. _____
5. _____
6. _____
7. _____
8. _____
9. _____
_____
_____

notes:

Magnetic Resonance Imaging (MRI)

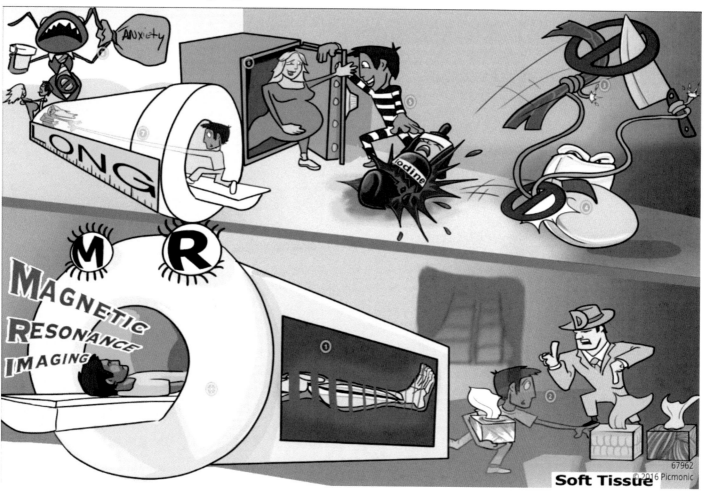

1. _____
2. _____
3. _____
4. _____
5. _____
6. _____
7. _____
8. _____
_____
_____
_____

notes:

Religion and Dietary Preferences Overview

1. _____
2. _____
3. _____
4. _____
5. _____
6. _____
7. _____
8. _____
9. _____
10. _____
11. _____
12.

notes:

5 Rights of Delegation

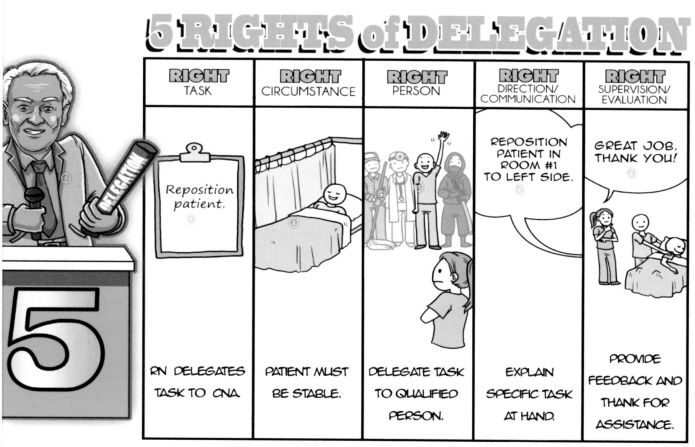

5 RIGHTS of DELEGATION

RIGHT TASK	RIGHT CIRCUMSTANCE	RIGHT PERSON	RIGHT DIRECTION/ COMMUNICATION	RIGHT SUPERVISION/ EVALUATION
Reposition patient.			REPOSITION PATIENT IN ROOM #1 TO LEFT SIDE.	GREAT JOB, THANK YOU!
RN DELEGATES TASK TO CNA.	PATIENT MUST BE STABLE.	DELEGATE TASK TO QUALIFIED PERSON.	EXPLAIN SPECIFIC TASK AT HAND.	PROVIDE FEEDBACK AND THANK FOR ASSISTANCE.

67962
© 2016 Picmonic

1. _____
2. _____
3. _____
4. _____
5. _____
_____
_____
_____
_____
_____
_____

notes:

Hypokalemia

1. _____
2. _____
3. _____
4. _____
5. _____
6. _____
7. _____
8. _____
9. _____
10. _____
_____

notes:

Hyperkalemia

1. _____
2. _____
3. _____
4. _____
5. _____
6. _____
7. _____
8. _____
9. _____
10. _____
_____

notes:

Hyponatremia

1. _____
2. _____
3. _____
4. _____
5. _____
6. _____
7. _____
8. _____
9. _____
10. _____

notes:

Hypernatremia

1. _____
2. _____
3. _____
4. _____
5. _____
6. _____
7. _____
8. _____
9. _____
10. _____
11. _____

notes:

Asthma Implementation and Education

1. _____
2. _____
3. _____
4. _____
5. _____
6. _____
7. _____
8. _____
9. _____
10. _____
_____

notes:

Tuberculosis Assessment

1. _____
2. _____
3. _____
4. _____
5. _____
6. _____
7. _____
8. _____
9. _____
10. _____
11. _____

notes:

COPD Overview (Chronic Obstructive Pulmonary Disease Overview)

1. _____
2. _____
3. _____
4. _____
5. _____
6. _____
7. _____
8. _____
_____
_____
_____

notes:

UTI Symptoms

1. _____
2. _____
3. _____
4. _____
5. _____
6. _____
7. _____
8. _____
9. _____
10. _____
11. _____

notes:

Loop Diuretics

1. _____
2. _____
3. _____
4. _____
5. _____
6. _____
7. _____
8. _____
9. _____
10. _____
11. _____

notes:

Hydrochlorothiazide HCTZ

© 2016 Picmonic

1. _____
2. _____
3. _____
4. _____
5. _____
6. _____
7. _____
8. _____
9. _____
10. _____
_____

notes:

Chronic Kidney Disease Interventions

1. _____
2. _____
3. _____
4. _____
5. _____
6. _____
7. _____
8. _____
9. _____
_____
_____

notes:

Hypertension Intervention

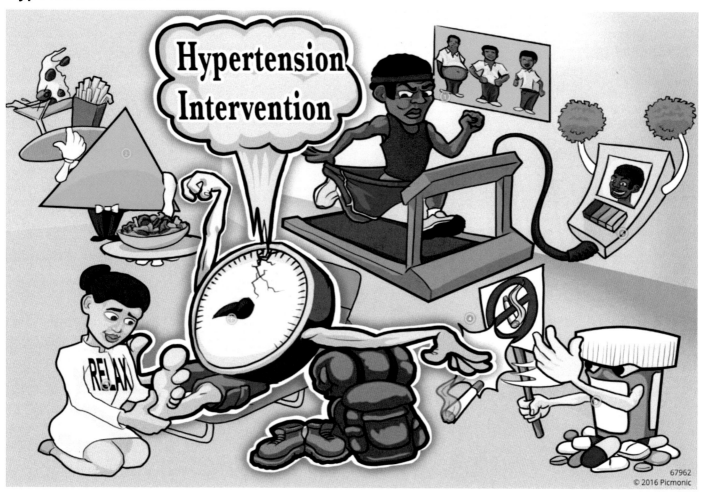

1. _____

2. _____

3. _____

4. _____

5. _____

6. _____

_____

_____

_____

_____

_____

notes:

Heart Failure Interventions

1. _____
2. _____
3. _____
4. _____
5. _____
6. _____
7. _____
8. _____
9. _____
10. _____
11. _____

notes:

Stable Angina

1. _____

2. _____

3. _____

4. _____

5. _____

6. _____

7. _____

8. _____

9. _____

_____

_____

notes:

Unstable Angina

1. _____
2. _____
3. _____
4. _____
5. _____
6. _____
7. _____
8. _____
_____
_____
_____

notes:

Warfarin (Coumadin)

1. _____
2. _____
3. _____
4. _____
5. _____
6. _____
7. _____
8. _____
9. _____
10. _____
_____

notes:

Hypertension Medications

1. _____

2. _____

3. _____

4. _____

5. _____

_____

_____

_____

_____

_____

notes:

Heparin (Unfractionated)

1. _____
2. _____
3. _____
4. _____
5. _____
6. _____
7. _____
8. _____
_____
_____
_____

notes:

Aspirin (Acetylsalicylic Acid)

1. _____
2. _____
3. _____
4. _____
5. _____
6. _____
7. _____
8. _____
9. _____
10. _____
11. _____

notes:

Hypoglycemia Assessment

HYPOGLYCEMIA ASSESSMENT

67962
© 2016 Picmonic

1. _____
2. _____
3. _____
4. _____
5. _____
6. _____
7. _____
8. _____
9. _____
10. _____
11. _____
12. _____

notes:

Hypoglycemia Intervention

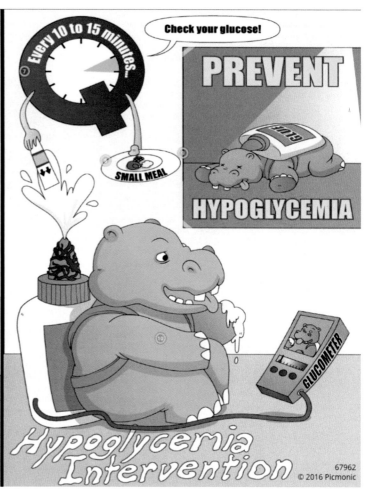

1. _____
2. _____
3. _____
4. _____
5. _____
6. _____
7. _____
8. _____
9. _____
10. _____
_____

notes:

Hypothyroidism Assessment

1. _____
2. _____
3. _____
4. _____
5. _____
6. _____
7. _____
8. _____
9. _____
10. _____
11. _____
12.

notes:

Diabetes Assessment

TYPE 1: JUVENILE ONSET

TYPE 2: ADULT ONSET

GESTATIONAL DIABETES

67962
© 2016 Picmonic

1. _____

2. _____

3. _____

4. _____

5. _____

6. _____

7. _____

8. _____

9. _____

10. _____

11. _____

12.

notes:

Levothyroxine (Synthroid)

© 2016 Picmonic

1. _____

2. _____

3. _____

4. _____

5. _____

6. _____

7. _____

8. _____

9. _____

_____

_____

notes:

Metformin (Glucophage)

1. _____
2. _____
3. _____
4. _____
5. _____
6. _____
7. _____
8. _____
9. _____
_____
_____

notes:

Hepatitis B (HBV) Assessment

1. _____
2. _____
3. _____
4. _____
5. _____
6. _____
7. _____
8. _____
9. _____
10. _____
_____

notes:

Gastroesophageal Reflux Disease (GERD) Assessment

1. _____
2. _____
3. _____
4. _____
5. _____
6. _____
7. _____
8. _____
9. _____
_____
_____

notes:

Cirrhosis Assessment

1. _____
2. _____
3. _____
4. _____
5. _____
6. _____
7. _____
8. _____
9. _____
_____
_____

notes:

Acute Pancreatitis Assessment

1. _____
2. _____
3. _____
4. _____
5. _____
6. _____
7. _____
8. _____
_____
_____
_____

notes:

Increased Intracranial Pressure (ICP) Interventions

1. _____
2. _____
3. _____
4. _____
5. _____
6. _____
7. _____
8. _____
9. _____
10. _____
_____

notes:

Parkinson's Disease Assessment

1. _____
2. _____
3. _____
4. _____
5. _____
6. _____
7. _____
8. _____
9. _____
_____
_____

notes:

Alzheimer's Disease Assessment (Early Symptoms)

1. _____
2. _____
3. _____
4. _____
5. _____
6. _____
_____
_____
_____
_____
_____

notes:

Seizure Precautions

1. _____
2. _____
3. _____
4. _____
5. _____
6. _____
7. _____

_____
_____
_____
_____

notes:

Phenytoin

1. _____
2. _____
3. _____
4. _____
5. _____
6. _____
7. _____
8. _____
9. _____
10. _____
11. _____
12. _____

notes:

Morphine

Benztropine (Cogentin)

1. _____
2. _____
3. _____
4. _____
5. _____
6. _____
7. _____
8. _____
9. _____
_____
_____

notes:

Naloxone (Narcan)

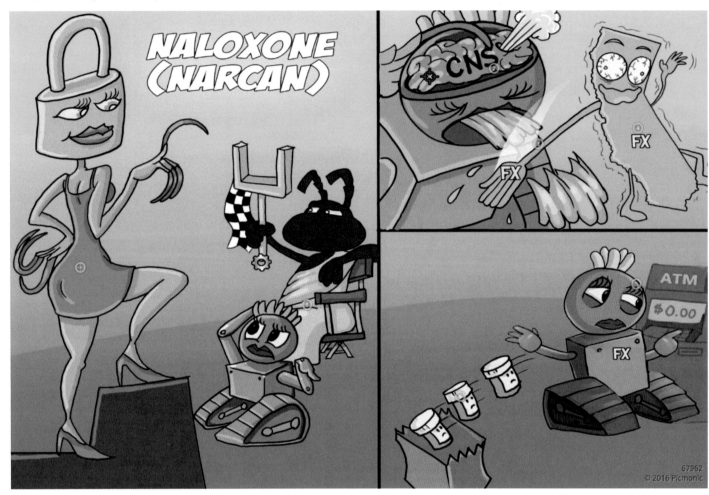

1. _____
2. _____
3. _____
4. _____
5. _____
6. _____

_____
_____
_____
_____

notes:

Venous Thromboembolism (DVT) Interventions

1. _____
2. _____
3. _____
4. _____
5. _____
6. _____
7. _____
_____
_____
_____
_____

notes:

Prostate Cancer Assessment

1. _____
2. _____
3. _____
4. _____
5. _____
6. _____
7. _____
8. _____
9. _____
_____
_____

notes:

Breast Cancer Diagnosis

© 2016 Picmonic

67962

1. _____

2. _____

3. _____

4. _____

5. _____

6. _____

7. _____

8. _____

9. _____

_____

_____

notes:

Venous Thromboembolism (DVT) Assessment

1. _____
2. _____
3. _____
4. _____
5. _____
6. _____
7. _____

_____
_____
_____
_____

notes:

Rheumatoid Arthritis Assessment

1. _____
2. _____
3. _____
4. _____
5. _____
_____
_____
_____
_____
_____
_____

notes:

Ibuprofen (Advil, Motrin)

1. _____
2. _____
3. _____
4. _____
5. _____
6. _____
7. _____
8. _____
9. _____
10. _____
_____

notes:

Prednisone (Glucocorticoids)

1. _____
2. _____
3. _____
4. _____
5. _____
6. _____
7. _____
8. _____
9. _____
10. _____
11. _____

notes:

Osteoporosis Interventions

Osteoporosis Interventions

67962
© 2016 Picmonic

1. _____
2. _____
3. _____
4. _____
5. _____
6. _____
7. _____
8. _____
9. _____
_____
_____

notes:

Compartment Syndrome Assessment

1. _____
2. _____
3. _____
4. _____
5. _____
6. _____
7. _____
8. _____
_____
_____
_____

notes:

Chest Tubes: Management and Care

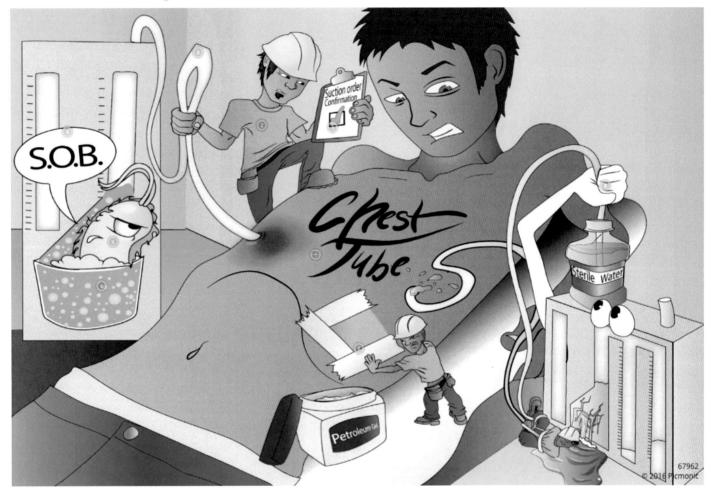

1. _____
2. _____
3. _____
4. _____
5. _____
6. _____
7. _____
8. _____
   _____
   _____
   _____

notes:

Preoperative Care

1. _____
2. _____
3. _____
4. _____
5. _____
6. _____
7. _____
8. _____
9. _____
10. _____
11. _____

notes:

Interventions for Impaired Skin Integrity

© 2016 Picmonic

1. _____
2. _____
3. _____
4. _____
5. _____
6. _____
7. _____
8. _____
9. _____
10. _____

notes:

Braden Scale

1. _____
2. _____
3. _____
4. _____
5. _____
6. _____

_____
_____
_____
_____
_____

notes:

Burns Interventions

1. _____
2. _____
3. _____
4. _____
5. _____
6. _____
7. _____
8. _____
9. _____
_____
_____

notes:

Vancomycin

1. _____
2. _____
3. _____
4. _____
5. _____
6. _____
7. _____
8. _____
9. _____
_____
_____

notes:

109

Penicillin

1. _____
2. _____
3. _____
4. _____
5. _____
6. _____
7. _____
8. _____
_____
_____
_____

notes:

Tetracyclines Overview

1. _____
2. _____
3. _____
4. _____
5. _____
6. _____
7. _____
   _____
   _____
   _____
   _____

notes:

Cephalosporins

1. _____
2. _____
3. _____
4. _____
5. _____
6. _____
7. _____
8. _____
9. _____
10. _____
_____

notes:

Preeclampsia Assessment

1. _____
2. _____
3. _____
4. _____
5. _____
6. _____
7. _____
8. _____

_____
_____
_____

notes:

RhoGam [Rho(D) Immune Globulin]

1. _____
2. _____
3. _____
4. _____
5. _____
6. _____
7. _____
8. _____
_____
_____
_____

notes:

Severe Preeclampsia

1. _____
2. _____
3. _____
4. _____
5. _____
6. _____
7. _____
8. _____
   _____
   _____
   _____

notes:

Eclampsia

1. _____
2. _____
3. _____
4. _____
5. _____
6. _____
7. _____
8. _____
9. _____
10. _____

notes:

Postpartum Nursing Assessment

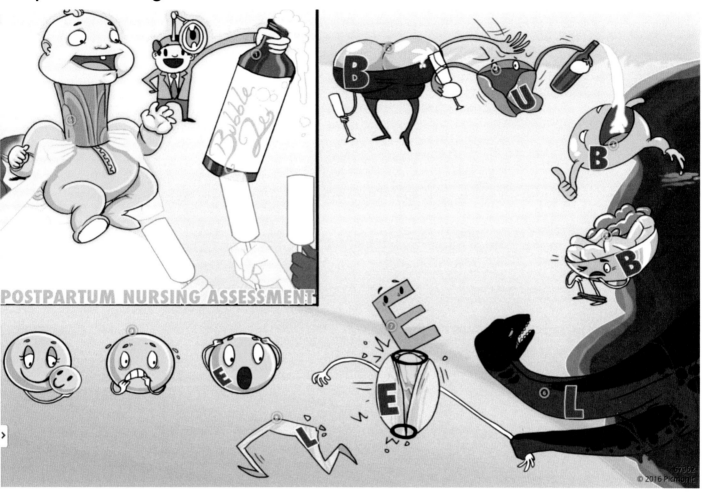

POSTPARTUM NURSING ASSESSMENT

© 2016 Picmonic

1. _____

2. _____

3. _____

4. _____

5. _____

6. _____

7. _____

8. _____

9. _____

_____

_____

notes:

Decelerations (and Accelerations) Overview

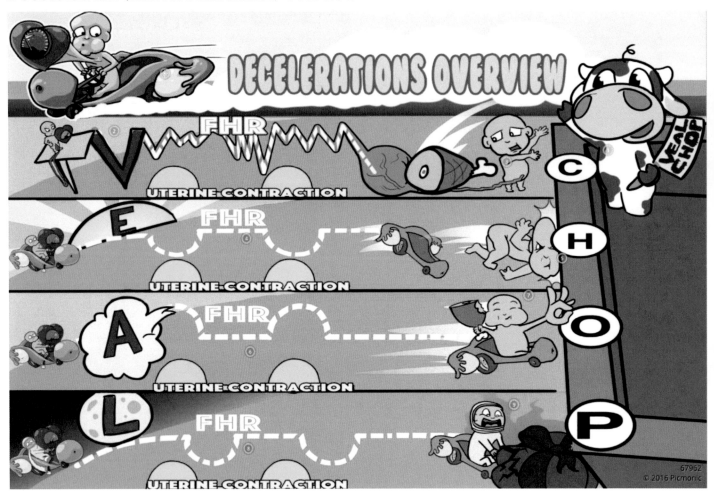

1. _____
2. _____
3. _____
4. _____
5. _____
6. _____
7. _____
8. _____
9. _____
_____
_____

notes:

Magnesium Sulfate

1. _____
2. _____
3. _____
4. _____
5. _____
6. _____
7. _____
8. _____
9. _____
10. _____
_____

notes:

Oxytocin (Pitocin)

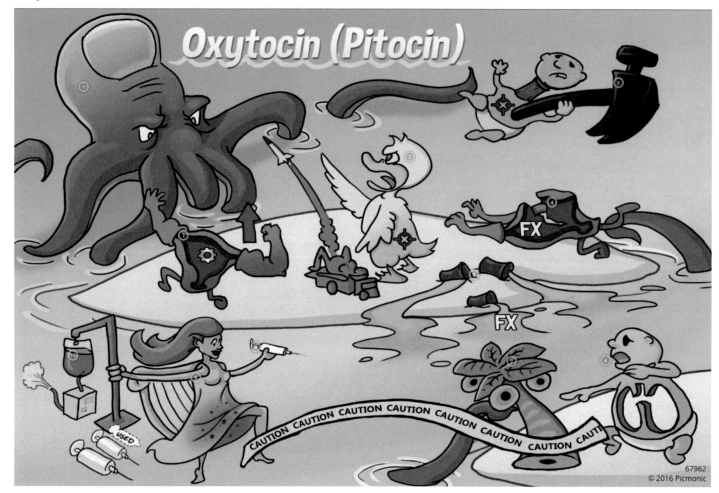

1. _____

2. _____

3. _____

4. _____

5. _____

6. _____

7. _____

8. _____

9. _____

10. _____

notes:

APGAR Score

1. _____
2. _____
3. _____
4. _____
5. _____
6. _____
7. _____
8. _____
9. _____
_____
_____

notes:

Age 2 Months - Developmental Milestones

1. _____
2. _____
3. _____
4. _____
5. _____

_____

_____

_____

_____

notes:

Age 6 Months - Developmental Milestones

1. _____
2. _____
3. _____
4. _____
5. _____
6. _____
7. _____
8. _____
_____
_____
_____

notes:

Age 9 Months - Developmental Milestones

1. _____
2. _____
3. _____
4. _____
5. _____
6. _____
7. _____
8. _____
   _____
   _____
   _____

notes:

Age 1 Year - Developmental Milestones

1. _____
2. _____
3. _____
4. _____
5. _____
6. _____
7. _____
8. _____
_____
_____
_____
_____

notes:

Respiratory Syncytial Virus (RSV) Assessment

© 2016 Picmonic

1. _____
2. _____
3. _____
4. _____
5. _____
6. _____
7. _____
8. _____
_____
_____
_____

notes:

Tetralogy of Fallot

1. _____
2. _____
3. _____
4. _____
5. _____
6. _____
7. _____
8. _____
9. _____
_____
_____

notes:

Schizophrenia Assessment

1. _____
2. _____
3. _____
4. _____
5. _____
6. _____
7. _____
8. _____
9. _____
_____
_____

notes:

Bipolar Disorder Assessment

1. _____
2. _____
3. _____
4. _____
5. _____
6. _____
7. _____
8. _____
9. _____
_____
_____

notes:

Suicide Assessment

1. _____
2. _____
3. _____
4. _____
5. _____
6. _____
7. _____
8. _____
9. _____
10. _____
11. _____
12.

notes:

Use of Restraints

1. _____
2. _____
3. _____
4. _____
5. _____
6. _____
7. _____
8. _____
_____
_____
_____

notes:

SIG E CAPS for Major Depressive Disorder (MDD)

1. _____

2. _____

3. _____

4. _____

5. _____

6. _____

7. _____

8. _____

9. _____

_____

_____

notes:

Neuroleptic Malignant Syndrome

1. _____
2. _____
3. _____
4. _____
5. _____
6. _____
7. _____
8. _____
9. _____
_____
_____

notes:

Benzodiazepine [Diazepam (Valium)]

1. _____
2. _____
3. _____
4. _____
5. _____
6. _____
7. _____
8. _____
9. _____
10. _____
11. _____
12.

notes:

Fluoxetine (Prozac)

1. _____
2. _____
3. _____
4. _____
5. _____
6. _____
7. _____
8. _____
9. _____
10. _____
_____

notes:

Clozapine (Clozaril)

1. _____
2. _____
3. _____
4. _____
5. _____
6. _____
7. _____
8. _____
9. _____
10. _____
11. _____

notes:

Benzodiazepine Antidote

1. _____
_____
_____
_____
_____
_____
_____
_____
_____
_____

notes:

Alcohol Abuse Interventions

1. _____
2. _____
3. _____
4. _____
5. _____
6. _____
7. _____
8. _____
9. _____
10. _____
_____

notes:

Opioid Abuse and Withdrawal Assessment

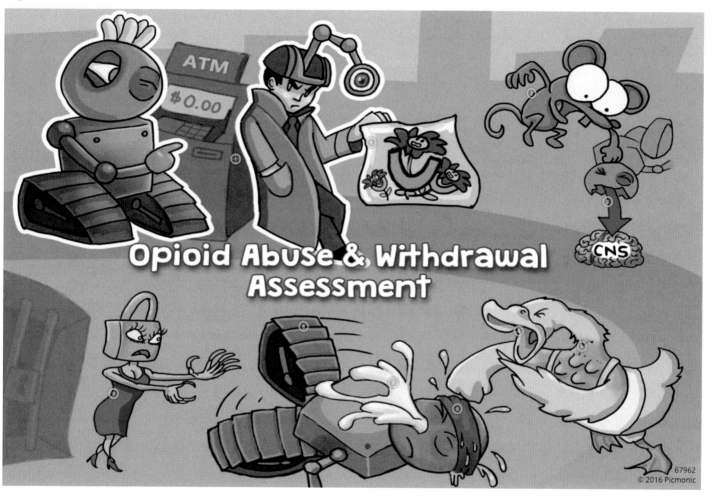

1. _____
2. _____
3. _____
4. _____
5. _____
6. _____
7. _____
8. _____
9. _____
_____
_____

notes:

WEEK 1

1) Fill in the Blank

1. 3.5-5.0 mEq/L
2. 15,3,8
3. 60-100
4. 8.5-10.5 mg/dL
5. Does not
6. Physiological
7. 135-145 mEq/L
8. Neutrophils
9. 13-7 g/dL, 12-16 g/dL
10. Negative
11. 1
12. Eosinophils
13. 10-14
14. 1.5- 2.5 mEq/L
15. 70-100 mg/dL
16. Surgeon
17. Sensory perception, moisture, activity, mobility, nutrition, friction and shear
18. 1 hour
19. Confin
20. Subcutaneous

2) Find the answers to the fill-in the Picmonics at
Picmonic.com

3) Question of the Day:

1) Respiratory Acidosis
Let's think about this for a second. Now let out a long sigh. Remember that when you breathe, you expel CO_2 (or acid). In this question, the patient has taken a few too many opiates, which causes respiratory depression. When patients don't breathe, they don't expel CO_2, and it builds up. In time, this leads to respiratory acidosis.

4) Match the Lung Sounds:

1) Wheezes, 2) Crackles 3) Rhonchi, 4) Pleural Friction Rub

WEEK 2

1) Insulin

Rapid Acting:
Insulin Lispro (Humalog):
Onset: 15-30 minutes
Duration: 3-6 hours

Insulin Aspart (Novolog):
Onset: 10-20 minutes
Duration: 3-5 hours

Insulin Glulisine (Apidra):
Onset: 10-15 min
Duration: 3-5 hours

Short Acting:
Regular Insulin (Humalin R):
Onset: 30-60 minutes
Duration: 6-10 hours

Intermediate Acting:
Isophane NPH (Humalin N):
Onset: 1-2 hours
Duration: 16-24 hours

Long Acting:
Detemir (Levemir):
Onset: 15-30 minutes
Duration: 3-6 hours

Glargine (Lantus):
Onset: 1 hour
Duration: One day

4) List 3 Differences Between Heparin and Warfarin

Heparin
Safe for pregnancy? Yes
Antidote: Protamine Sulfate
What to monitor: aPTT
Warfarin
Safe for pregnancy? No
Antidote: Vitamin K and Fresh Frozen Plasma
What to monitor: INR

cations to this

ated in patients,
ısly through
e solutions
, dextrose,
Additional
) the TPN solu-
d through the
aration should
ırge central
such as throm-
rapidly, TPN
e nausea and
iuresis. Do not
pt to catch up if
ınd remember,
PN infusions.

Question of the Day:

3) Niacin

Niacin (B3) is indicated to raise HDL levels. It clas-
sically can cause a "niacin flush" or flushed skin
after administration. You can always remember this
because the popular energy drinks, "5 Hour Energy"
have 2000% of your daily required intake of Niacin,
and you guessed it...there's a warning on the label
that states "may cause skin flushing." Nursing ge-
nius.

7) All Things Blood Crossword Puzzle Answer Key

1) Fill in the Blank

1. 18%
2. 9%
3. 24 hours
4. Compression
5. Serosanguineous
6. Benzodiazepines
7. Should not
8. Dopamine
9. Agnosia, Anomia, Aphasia, Apraxia, Amnesia
10. Thrombotic and embolic

2) Question of the Day

ANSWER: 2, 3

Genital herpes is caused by types 1 and 2 of the
herpes simplex virus (HSV), although HSV type 2 is
typically responsible for genital infections in both
men and women. Lesions or "fever blisters" may appear on the oral mucosa, or in this case, the genitals.
Lesions are usually small and vesicular. They can be
painful; however, painless lesions may also appear
on infected sites. Painless chancres are a characteristic of syphilis, not herpes. It's important to remember that patients are infectious during recurrences
of the infection, which may be triggered by stress,
fatigue, sunburn, acute illness, immunosuppression,
and menses. Prodromal symptoms include tingling, burning, and itching at the site where lesions
typically reappear. Penicillin is usually given as a
treatment for syphilis, while antivirals such as acy-
clovir, valacyclovir, and famciclovir are often used to
reduce outbreaks/recurrences or treat infections.

6) Question of the Day:

1) Avocados, 2) Spinach 3) Potatoes
Patients at risk for hypokalemia, such as those on
diuretics, should understand the importance of
eating a balanced diet and including foods high in
potassium. Examples of foods high in potassium are
avocados, spinach, and potatoes. The other options
here are low in potassium.

7) Match the Antibiotic with Possible Side Effects

Vancomycin	Red man syndrome
Tetracyclines	Bone deformities and discoloration of teeth

Macrolides	QT prolongation
Fluoroquinolnes	Achilles tendon rupture
Cephalosporins	Thrombophlebitis during IV infusion

WEEK 4
1) Fill in the Blank
Probable
1. Presumptive
2. 1 and 5 minutes
3. Moderate distress
4. E=Elevated L=Liver Enzymes
5. Side-lying
6. Placenta previa
7. Six months
8. One year
9. Intussusception

2) Match the Psychiatric Disorder

Obsessive Compulsive Disorder	Anxiety about losing control, has repetitive, intrusive thoughts that interfere with daily functioning
Post Traumatic Stress Disorder	Re-experiences traumatic events, is avoidant, and has self-destructive behaviors
Bipolar Disorder	When manic, has nonstop physical activity, rapid speech, flight of ideas, and euphoric mood
Schizophrenia	Has flat affect, hallucinations or delusions, illogical thinking, impaired judgment or memory
Illusion	Misinterpretation of stimulus
Delusions	A fixed, false belief
Hallucinations	No external stimulus
Borderline Personality Disorder	Has chronic feelings of emptiness, poor self-image, self-destructive behaviors and is unable to maintain stable relationships
Antisocial Personality Disorder	Disregards the rights of others, often manipulative and lacks remorse for actions

3) Question of the Day:
2. If I miss a dose of this medication I should double up the next dose.
Lithium has a narrow therapeutic range, therefore serum levels should be monitored and patients should never double up on these types of medications. As a general rule, you should never tell a patient to double up their medication dosages. Lithium also has an unknown mechanism of action and does not directly act on serotonin receptors. While it's a good idea to frequently check blood pressure, it's not required. Remember, it's asking which statement indicates a need for further education, meaning we are looking for the incorrect answers. Lithium is contraindicated in pregnancy and has side effects of tremors, SIADH, and hypothyroidism.

3. Because this medication works on my serotonin receptors, I will be sure to let my doctor know if there is an increase or decrease in blood pressure and check it weekly.

6) Crossword: Need To Know Pharmacology For the NCLEX

142

GRAM-NEG

DIPLOCOCCI
DOUBLE-COCKEYES

MALTOSE-FERMENTER
MALT-LIQUOR FERN

MALTOSE NON-FERMENTER
NUN WITH MALT-LIQUOR FERN

NEISSERIA GONORRHOEAE
KNIVES GUNNER-SHIP

NEISSERIA MENINGITIDIS
KNIVES MEN-IN-TIGHTS

GRAM-NEGATIVE

144

COCCOID RODS
COCK-EYED RODS

BORDETELLA PERTUSSIS
BORDER.PEARL-TUSK

BRUCELLA
BRUCE-LEE

HAEMOPHILUS INFLUENZAE
HE-MAN FLUTE

GRAM-NEGATIVE

PASTEURELLA
PASTA-RELLA

145

OXIDASE-POSITIVE COMMA-SHAPED
OX-DAISY (POSITIVE) AND COMMA-SHAPED SHRIMP

HELICOBACTER PYLORI
HELICOPTER BACTERIA

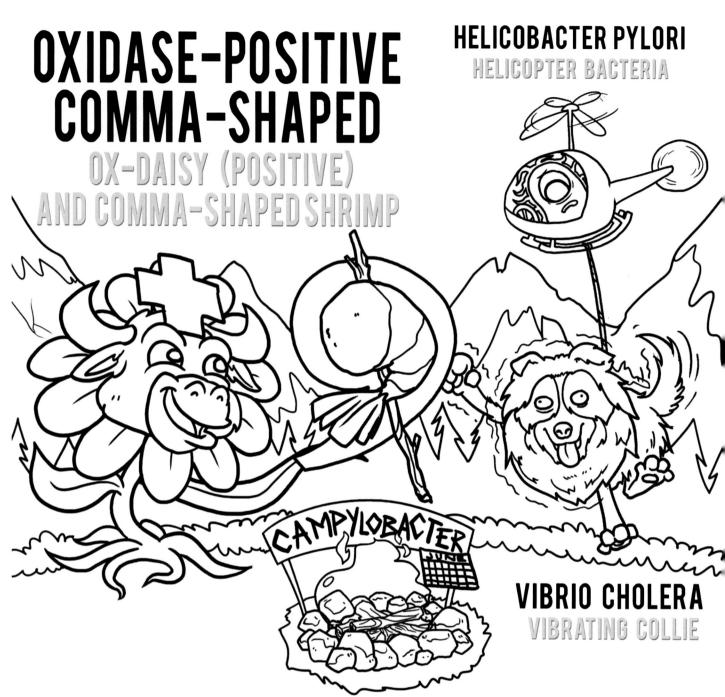

VIBRIO CHOLERA
VIBRATING COLLIE

CAMPYLOBACTER JEJEUNI
CAMPING SCENE IN (JEJEUNI) JUNE

GRAM-NEGATIVE

BACILLI
RODS

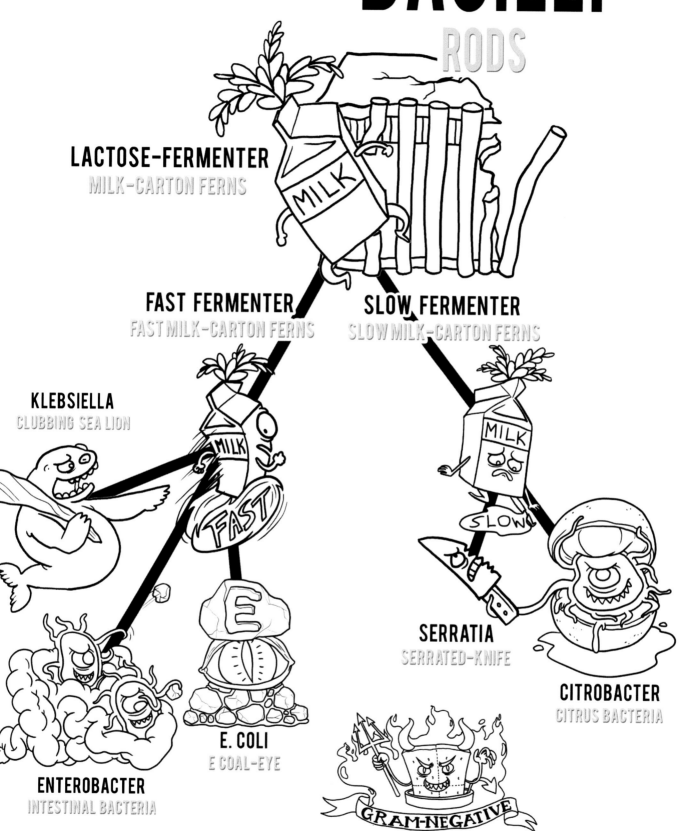

LACTOSE-FERMENTER
MILK-CARTON FERNS

FAST FERMENTER
FAST MILK-CARTON FERNS

SLOW FERMENTER
SLOW MILK-CARTON FERNS

KLEBSIELLA
CLUBBING SEA LION

SERRATIA
SERRATED-KNIFE

CITROBACTER
CITRUS BACTERIA

ENTEROBACTER
INTESTINAL BACTERIA

E. COLI
E COAL-EYE

GRAM-NEGATIVE

BACILLI
RODS

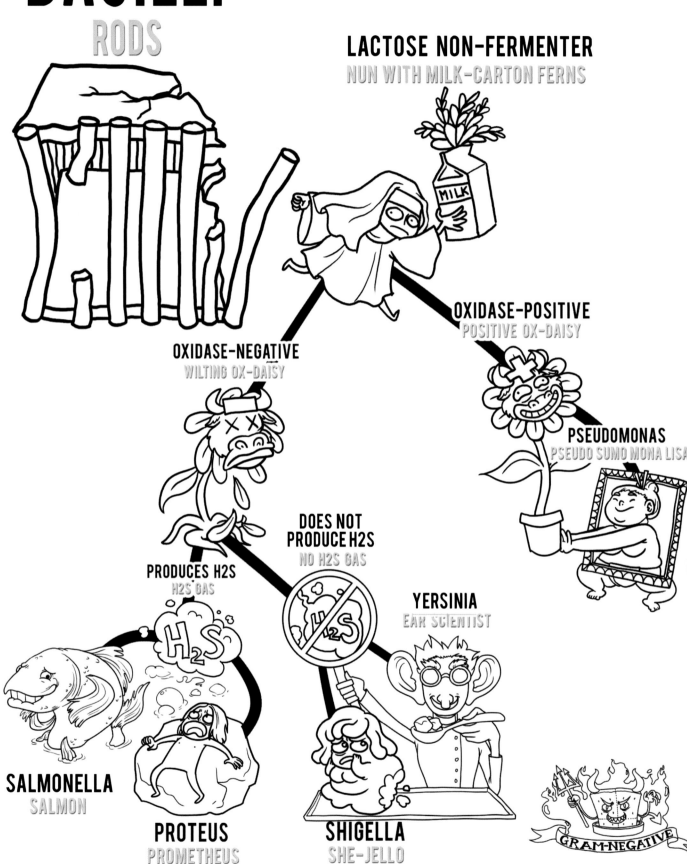

LACTOSE NON-FERMENTER
NUN WITH MILK-CARTON FERNS

OXIDASE-POSITIVE
POSITIVE OX-DAISY

OXIDASE-NEGATIVE
WILTING OX-DAISY

PSEUDOMONAS
PSEUDO SUMO MONA LISA

DOES NOT PRODUCE H2S
NO H2S GAS

PRODUCES H2S
H2S GAS

YERSINIA
EAR SCIENTIST

SALMONELLA
SALMON

PROTEUS
PROMETHEUS

SHIGELLA
SHE-JELLO

GRAM-NEGATIVE

148

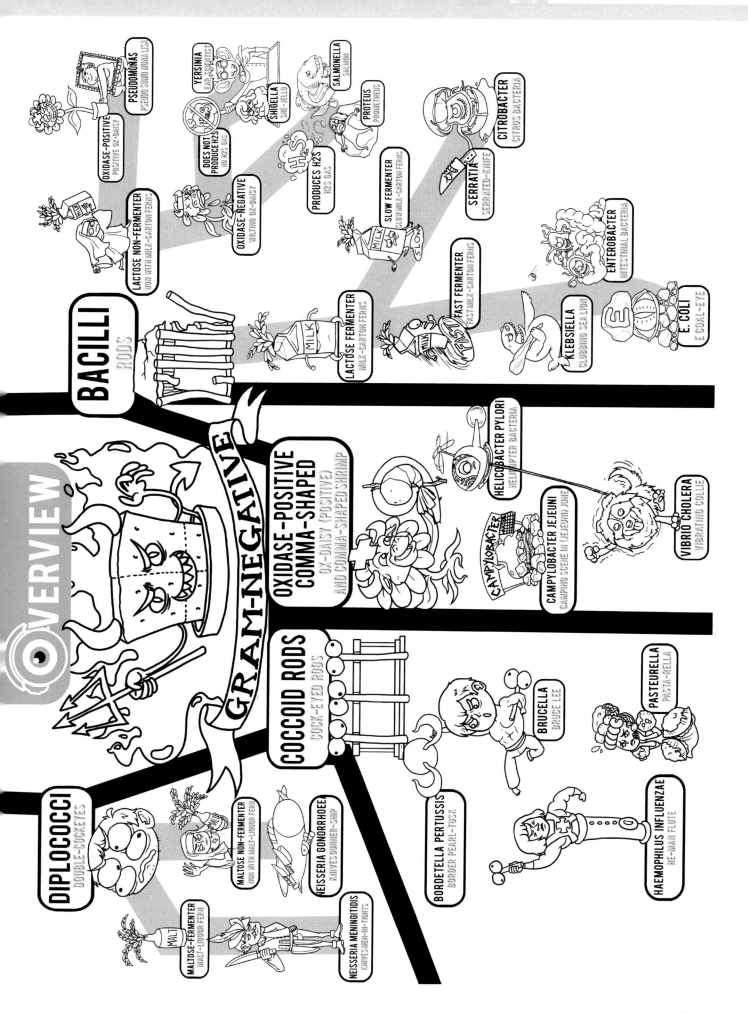

Beta Blockers
(Beta-fish with Blocks)

Warfarin
(War-fairy)

MAXIMIZE YOUR MEMORY.

Thank you for studying with us!

Here it is! The end of the workbook. You put forth so much time and effort and learned so much along the way. We hope you found studying with Picmonic not only only useful and simple to use but enjoyable as well. Now with our unforgettable characters by your side, you can take on the NCLEX ® with confidence! Want additional tips? Check out our "How to Pass the NCLEX® the First Time with Picmonic" on Youtube for some last minute tips and pointers for your big day.

We wish you the best of luck! Let us know how you did!

The Picmonic Team
feedback@picmonic.com

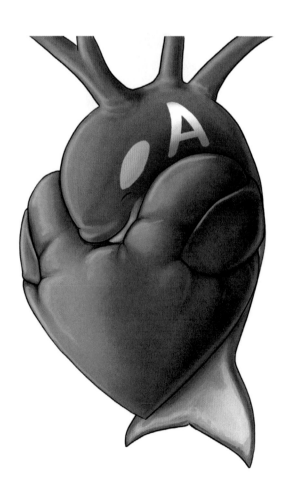

PICMONIC DOG & CAT TAX

Penny
Likes lettuce, hates fork

Sir Kota Bear
Really really ridiculously good looking

Macy
Can eat a whole banana

Miss Maya
Touch me and I'll kill you

Huxley
Zero hux to give

Eddie
Netflix & chills

Dr. Dubby & Nurse Tula
Bone specialists

Lil' Señor
Big heart

King Cheese Louie
Judging you

Albie
Loves pillows, hates the toaster

Lando Dogrissian
Master of the puppy dog eyes

Tot
Destroyer of kale

Mochi
Rap name T. Mo

Beefcake
Rap name B. Flo

Hunter
Certified Fluffalo

Tyrion Hammister
Dwarf hamster of Hamster-ly rock

NOTES:

NOTES:

NOTES:

NOTES:

Made in the USA
Middletown, DE
31 March 2022

63413943R00088